summer of pure ice

by

William White

Dragon's Teeth Press
El Dorado National Forest
Georgetown, California 95634

SUMMER OF PURE ICE

Published by Dragon's Teeth Press, El Dorado National Forest, Georgetown, California 95634. Manufactured in the United States of America.

LIMITED FIRST EDITION

LIBRARY OF CONGRESS Catalogue Card Number: 84-70670

ILLUSTRATIONS: by John Aracco

LIVING POETS SERIES, Number 29
Available at $5.00 per copy
from:

Dragon's Teeth Press
El Dorado National Forest
Georgetown, California 95634

ISBN: 0-934218-29-3

ACKNOWLEDGMENTS

Some of the poems in the collection have previously appeared in the following publications, to which grateful acknowledgment is made: *Black Willow, Berkley Poetry Review, Blue Buildings, Colorado-North Review, Folio, New Kent Quarterly, Poetry Newsletter, Poetry View, Quartet, Southwest Review, Swallow's Tale, Texas Review, Wisconsin Review, and Zahir*. Thanks are due to several of the editors for permission to reprint.

The poems "Susan Upon the Rock," "Susan Upon Her Bed," and "Susan at the Gate" originally appeared in the Spring, 1977 issue of the *Southern Review*. "Susan's Journey" originally appeared in the April, 1979 issue of the *Southern Review*. "Summer of Pure Ice" originally appeared in the Summer, 1980 issue of the *Southern Review*. "Inside the Wind" and "Palm Beach in August" originally appeared in the Summer, 1982 issue of *The Southern Review*. "After the Killing" originally appeared in a 1984 issue of *The Southern Review*.

"Audrey," "Susan's Journey," "Summer of Pure Ice" and "From the Porch" were published as a thirty-page chapbook, FROM THE PORCH, Chase Avenue Press, 1983, Winter Park, Florida.

CONTENTS

V. MEDLEY

I. WOMEN KNOWN AND UNKNOWN

AFTER THE PARTY

A man frightens his house
by screaming and throwing a sofa
He knocks holes in the plaster
and rapes his drunken wife
while the girl-child watches
with a cloud in her brain

The child does not hear
when he stomps and thunders
roaring throughout the house
She watches upon the neck
of a newly broken beer bottle
two red-backed flies at mating

Her father's voice
dark sound of boulders
strikes cold against her ear
She wishes to pluck roses
her thin arms lifting
to the pit of the sky

The man and the woman stand forth
as though newly born to her
and step out of their shells
stark white   pocked with red
stone white   spotted with red
skin white   flayed with red

The child hides and curls in a corner
while it moves throughout the house   the sound
printing the red   printing the black
cracking and breaking the shell of her

She can hear her mother's skin
as it soaks and dries   deep in the linen
and she can see light in a hanging rose

INSIDE THE WIND

In dresses too short for school
they run on thin brown legs
down to the tracks by the river

Each day they crouch in the ditch
arms tight around narrow waists
as the train breaks out of its tunnel
and kisses their arms with a gritty wind

At the end of a long summer
they string their dolls to the track
and kneel in the low ditch
to whisper about a blond boy
who lives in a shack by the river

Jackdaws start out of trees
flashing their silver necks
as the rails hum loud
and they lean into the bank
arms hugged around their knees
to wait for the coming wind

FROM THE PORCH

Margaret I speak to you
in my bold gravelly voice
about the anatomy of a horse's leg
and of how my boots can gallop

Poor Margaret I cry for you
like a preacher with soft hands
or like your own lost children
who roam in the big forest

Let us move inside this night
away from the chill that hovers
and hide my face between your hands
with their quick bones so grasping

Shall we listen--shall we wait
as you are fond of telling me
in that firm sweet voice of yours
for those good things yet beginning

Night air tempts me from our porch
to seek a warmth that ought to be
as I reach beneath my hoofprints
for the hard and barren ground

Margaret I hear a wreck out there
down corner from the orange light
the grinding crash and then a squeal
from a wild thing caught at dying

AFTER THE KILLING

next morning   alive with its memory
      we huddled at the breakfast table
      contemplating our eggs our words talking softly
      after washing our hands with powdered soap

There was nothing in the spread open newspaper
or in the dark closet at the end of a hall
or in the car out back   no bloody trunk
      nothing as real or obvious as that
but someone had died like others that went before

When a tossed stone ripples a millpond
the circle spreads   lingers a moment
then all is flat and calm again   serene
      as though it never dared to be

We shove back the dishes   empty now
And bend our necks to lean our heads across our arms
as sunshine enters an open window high above the streets
      to warm our sleepy eyes

After the killing it was calm   a spring-like day
limp and lazy as a sleeping dog   till a breeze hit
      and rattled teacups in a tall red cabinet
So staunch behind us against the wall

POSTED

Light sprays through a dirty transom
onto someone posted in shadows
in the back corner of an empty room

When I look between the legs
I discover that it's a young woman
statued on the glassy floor

She is coated with flakes of metal
except for her face--she has no face

As the light grows brighter
the metal whirs away to cluster
just above her stiff black hair

She stands naked in a rising light
and I see large purple breasts
turgid with their sullen blood

Her yellow thighs are thick with fat
between rigid arms extended

Just now I see her face--her angry eyes
as the metal swoops down to hover
before spreading out to cover her

When the metal swirls once more
to group beneath the transom
her position has changed

Now she is bent low
with knees pressed against her cheeks
and the light grows within her eyes

MY LADY

Think how you emptied
the sea from inside me
and fixed me with your eyes
while you drained me
day after living day
till I drifted to Calcutta
like a piece of wood
caught in your bold current

Here are the hands you cut off
when they reached out for you
Hands that washed up
against your shore
like parched dead fish
with white wafer bones

Oh I do not reclaim deadness
You may tuck them in your pocket
as a final gift from me

I would rather walk now
on a lower solid ground
with two whole feet
and make-believe hands
than to live again with you
in a drowning that has no end
I would rather sit alone
on the edge of the world
and whistle at the sea
as a gull floats
free within my vacant eye

SUSAN'S JOURNEY

A butler brought in the package
--in a meduim-sized box
Placed it on the table
It contained seven pounds of rich black dirt
And one grass seed beginning to sprout
No one bothered to open it

A butler brought in the package
--in a small-sized box
Placed it on the table
It contained a black-lace garter belt
An attached pair of silk stockings
No one bothered to open it

A butler brought in the package
--in a medium-sized box
Placed it on the table
It contained a pleated white shirt
The buttons ripped off its front
No one bothered to open it

A butler brought in the package
--in a large-sized box
Placed it on the table
It contained a seven-pound baby
Squalling and thrashing its fists
No one bothered to open it

The butler died

A yardman brought in the package
--in a medium-sized box
Placed it on the table
It contained a rubber doll in a plaid skirt
Its chest bare and cheeks smeared with rouge
Its eyes coated over with mildew
No one bothered to open it

A yardman brought in the package
--in a medium-sized box
Placed in on the table
It contained three thin books
A dried white carnation
A cigarette lighter that leaked fluid
And a week-old calico kitten
No one bothered to open it

A yardman brought in the package
--in a medium-sized box
Placed it on the table
It contained a dead pale canary
With a large blackbird
Perched on its small chest
No one bothered to open it

A yardman brought in the package
--in a small-sized box
Placed in on the table
It contained three minnows forming a triangle
With black ants swarming atop them
No one bothered to open it

A yardman brought in the package
--in a large-sized box
Placed it on the table
It contained a leather riding crop
An enormous sun-ripened watermelon
That had exploded into zigzag pieces
No one bothered to open it

The yardman died

A delivery boy brought in the package
--in a meduim-sized box
Placed it on the table
It contained a packet of yellow capsules
A cream-colored douche bag
A passport and a ring engraved on the inside
No one bothered to open it

A delivery boy brought in the package
--in a large-sized box
Placed it on the table
It contained a pint half full of tequila
A quarter of a shriveled lemon
A salt shaker and a stuffed iguana
No one bothered to open it

A delivery boy brought in the package
--in a medium-sized box
Placed it on the table
It contained two purple satin sheets
Two stained pillow cases
And a small jar of holy water
No one bothered to open it

The delivery boy died

A neighbor brought in the package
--in a medium-sized box
Placed it on the table
It contained a mink coat with sweaty armpits
No one bothered to open it

A neighbor brought in the package
--in a medium-sized box
Placed it on the table
It contained a bible in gold-leaf
A jar of dried-up skin cream
And two broken silver bracelets
No one bothered to open it

A neighbor brought in the package
--in a medium-sized box
Placed it on the table
It contained two decks of playing cards
Some tulip bulbs
And get-well wishes in a rubber band
No one bothered to open it

A neighbor brought in the package
--in a large-sized box
Placed it on the table
It contained three mixed-breed cats
Curled up asleep in a circle
No one bothered to open it

The neighbor died

There was a package
--in a medium-sized box
Placed on the table
It contained seven pounds of rich black dirt
And one grass seed beginning to sprout

IN ANOTHER SEASON

That day I had made
A hay-drop from the helicopter
To a starving doe
Waist-deep in the snow frozen
Across Virginia at twilight

I saw her sniff and lumber forward
Drunk upon her stiffened legs
And I was glad

Later that evening
There was a hollow-cheeked girl
With deep scratches down the backs
Of both her long-long legs
Fresh scratches running from thigh to ankle
These dripping streaks
As though she ripped herself on wire
Too low to crawl beneath

She did not mention them
As we sat close on leather stools
Drinking beer from thick mugs
Our elbows touching

In fact she never spoke at all
Climbed down and walked away
Into the coldness of night
With those bright red rivulets
Flowing the length of her pale-white legs

LITTLE RED SCHOOLHOUSE

We closed up the castle
with pounding tambourines
We manage
We manage

Tallboy stands in his corner
Sent there by short teacher
His back quivers bone
We play him by shaking
by striking with the hand

Your initials are beneath my fist
A knifed heart encasing them
I scissor your head from the back row
of big-eyed girls with hair like yours
and lose it from my pocket playing
King On The Mountain

You whisper spell words in my ear
Never knew you then or now
Lost your head from pocket
Lost all their heads--year after year
till I reopened the castle
with pounding tambourines

CLARA ANNE

You tiptoe our living room
and linger your fingerstrokes
along the surface of wooden things

Slowly you dance that rhythm
playing strangely in your head
to where I lie in shadows
atop an eight-foot couch

When you pass by you stop
look down and almost see me
before you glide to pause
beside the blue aquarium

Five large black angel fish
rise to the top so quickly
and open their oval mouths

You come to me with honey
to stand in gentle light
Your gown swirls my cheek
and I float toward surfaces
as I close my eyes and wait

RED ROVER-RED ROVER

The girls wore white miniskirts
with pleats at the funeral
and dirty satin underpants
that barely covered their asses

They circle-danced the coffin
Leaped the carpeted mound of dirt
Bowed and clapped three times

"His name was Biff the Stiff --
Whata funny name" someone said
They giggled and twisted
and tossed their jet-black hair

"He was a people" the Parson said
"At eighteen
the apple of Calvary"

Parson pointed to the girl in jeans
swollen beneath her blouse
"He left a wife
or a lover
or something or other"

Sunlight stirred her to motion
She writhed atop the casket
moaned a bit
popped out the baby
fell asleep in a heap

They danced around the coffin
Blonde hair swirling
in long black dresses
that swished the icy ground

The baby squalled
when the umbilical cord was cut
with a rusty girl-scout knife
that the Parson borrowed

"It's a people" the Parson said
"Can't even see yet
Not even buried yet --
And yet we welcome
this chubby cherub
A child it is" he said
"The son of Calvary"

AFTER LETTING GO

The pain inside my bones is an echo
of that which saved--Oh Lord--so many times
and the people standing on my chest
are heavy as a ceiling hung with light

This startled flesh of stone
this shield of metal bright
and the cost to me--Oh Helen
the dear-dear cost to me

You stand there breathing
with the throat of a pale bird
as I watch your silent fingers
talk of this and nothing more

While open in a sunlit land
little girls with gapped smiles
lie back on pine needles
to look at tree tops rising

Flesh of stone and ceiling bright
a pain inside my bones so many times
as you bake a loaf of tuesday bread
swaying in the softest light
and meet each lifted morning
with a warm and gentle kiss

II. SUMMER OF PURE ICE

SUMMER OF PURE ICE

In July of 1941 at Bowling Green
Jutting above river water an ice factory
Where we drove each dawn in blue pick-up
Backed up to loading platform

Purified mud water from river piped up
And frozen inside molds in an upper room
Then swirling down ramp as block of ice
A trunk-shaped three-hundred-pound "can"
Clanging through the rusty cutting machine
Which sawed lines for picking

Then climbing onto platform with ice hooks
Where we slide each can inside truck's bed
Line them together in a sunrise column
Cover with heavy-green tarpaulin
Ready for the day's run

Me swaying on hanging metal backstep
Inches above the bouncing road
Maynard driving with his one arm
Whipping the truck with that skull knob
Lifting knees against wheel to shift gears
Or tug his cap lower

His left arm missing below elbow
Stump safety-pinned inside workshirt sleeve
Because a coal truck flipped on Morgantown Pike
And cut it off so surgeon-clean that
His strength flowed straight into the right arm
Till he could jerk 100 pounds with ice hook
Swing it high overhead in a soft arc
And splash it down in a wooden water barrel
Almost without breathing

Sometimes he would ask me to stiffen arms together
In front of my crotch with hands flat pressed
A too-big teenager lifted with palm of right hand
From underneath into sky above his head
Then eased back down again

He was my uncle's best "hand" of the three
Delivering coal in winter and ice in summer
From sunrise to sunset for a dollar a day
Year in and year out--seven days a week
Except for me working for the fun of it
To pass a summer vacation

Bardell dipped snuff and had nine children
Fat Howard sweated and talked real mean
Couldn't read or write or things like that
Scrawled their big X marks slowly in pencil
Except for Maynard--I taught him on a Sunday
To print his full name

We would joggle along in our old International
Down the gravel or dirt streets in a pattern
And spot each ice card in front windows
Pinned to thin curtains or stuck above plants
Showing 25-or 50-or 75-or 100 pounds
By the corner turned up

Most paid us in frayed cardboard tickets
Bought in advance to save pennies
A different color for each sized cake of ice
And some paid us with buffalo nickels
Which were being replaced by shiny Jeffersons
Because Maynard said buffaloes shit in your pocket
And pissed down your leg

Each afternoon I'd sort the day's coins
Drop them into paper rollers for the bank
Count the colored tickets to add it all up
For my uncle who couldn't see good any more
And was so proud of my arithmetic and the way
I double-checked it all

Under 50 pounds Maynard would let me tote
To ice boxes which were damp-cabbage smelly
And I had to move bottles and squishy things
To force room for the beautiful new ice
While the women dumped out drip pans
Telling me "Watch out for this or watch out
For that and don't track those muddy feet
On my clean linoleum"

Some of the houses had dirt floors
Others had rickety outside stairs
With rotting boards and loose railings
With the ice chafing red spots against my leg
And soaking my pants and shoes so soggy cold
That they never dried in the sun

Kids trotted behind us begging chips of ice
And I'd reach and toss some when we stopped
Holding the truck's metal side with my left hand
Throwing my ice pick "twang" with my right
Where it would quiver in the wooden platform
Of the soft-wet truckbed

Then I would take my hooks and prance off
Pretending that 50 pounds was not heavy
While Maynard would stand with the kids
And twist their ears hard if they were boys
And stroke their asses tender if they were girls
Before he'd give each one a chip of clear ice
To crunch and suck on

Sometimes Maynard would stay in a house so long
I'd worry and go peek through the open door
And see him with a woman backed against a wall
Her dress hem tucked up tight under her chin
And him standing so close against her front
Moving back and forth and making a noise
Like dogs that chased our truck when I kicked them
To stop that yelping

When I could see the women they'd be smiling
Or sometimes just blank-looking into air
And often they'd bite their lips with eyes shut
Or now and then one would see me watching her
And stick out her tongue at me

I never told Maynard what I saw through the doors
Or over the windowsills--though he did it in plain sight
Over against the wall with all his clothes and cap on
And sometimes the women would have kids crawling
Near their feet and yelling for things--but they stood
With their backs to the wall and their dresses hiked up
With their eyes shut while they moaned and smiled
And kept their feet so still

Then he would come out whistling or shaking his head
And we'd drive off with me sitting next to him
To handle the money--'cause I kept the sack
Or the colored tickets--and he'd tell me "Forget that one
I took it out in trade"

Course I wasn't sure what "it" was
Only that he'd whistle happy songs
Like "Old Gray Mare Ain't What She Used to Be"
Then reach over and squeeze my leg fierce hard
Till I yelled outloud--and he'd tell me
"Don't ever let me catch you doing that 'cause
You might get aholt of something you couldn't
Get loose of"

When I took in 50 pounds to a woman
Later that summer it happened
With her two kids shooting rubber guns at my head
The kind where you whittle it like a pistol
Out of an inch-thick piece of soft wood
Then strap a clothes pin firm behind the handle
Stretch them tight from pin to barrel tip
And then press down the trigger and shoot them
Zing from your gun

So when I shoved the 50 pounds in the old sour box
The kids shot me and laughed and ran out the backdoor
Just as the mother called from the other room
For me to come and collect

She was standing there naked when I opened the door
"Got no money today" she said "Not a blessed cent"
She was saggy fat and dirty-hairy looking
And had on nothing but pink bedroom slippers
"Come get it now" she said "Ain't got all day for this"
Brown stuff drooled from the corner of her mouth
"Doncha know how--come here to me" she said
"I gonna hafta learn you"

I ran out to our truck and sent Maynard inside
But he came right back with her ice card tucked
Under the stump of his arm and spat in the dust
"Don't take that one no more ice" he said
"She ain't worth a nickel--much less fifteen cents
She got no money or nothing else in there
I want no part of

"Paid cash till her old man took off last week
But now I'm gonna cut her from our list"
We climbed in the cab "What a rat's ass" he said
"Wouldn't stick my stump in that" Pinched his nose shut
With his fingers "Phew--whee--don't blame him for leaving"
He said "He's lucky gone"

That's how it was back then--hard times for folks
Lots of flat tires and cold-patching the innertubes
Dirty kids looking mean-lonely in the yellow sunshine
Lots of people eating Campbell's tomato soup and crackers
With baloney or sardines

The little Irish lady I liked so much
Gave me oatmeal cookies and paid for her ice
In pennies she untied from a kerchief all knotted up
That took her forever to undo while I ate my cookies
Till she died one weekend and the shades were down
And her ice card was gone

Lots of talk about the weather--lots of faded shirts
With holes in them and grease-stained pants and grimy dresses
And streaked cheeks and matted hair in the sunshine
And the rough roads with kids and dogs trotting
Behind me in swirling dust

Maynard teasing the kids whenever we parked our truck
And that great way he had of swinging ice over his head
And talking about "it" and how I'd get some
Any day now and me bouncing along on my backstep
Of our old International and remembering that dirty woman
With her brown mouth and thick hair on her belly
And knowing that she wasn't yet the "it"
To make me whistle

It was standing in the sun or perching high in the cab
Watching him spin that skull around when we cornered
It was the dirt roads in the heat and the beautiful cans
Of new ice sliding each dawn from the cutting machine
And all the shiny coins and colored tickets and ice cards
That the kids sucked on while running behind
My wet pants leg as I stood with my back to them all
Frozen and waiting

III. ALONE WITH SELF AND OTHERS

NIGHTLIGHTS

When I spot dead boy-men
or the dead girl-women
sprawled in my bright lights
along the road shoulder
run over and crushed so many times
that often I can't distinguish them
from pigs or large dogs
I dim my lights and do not try

They frolic in the big woods
and sleep all day upon leaves
When they dart naked onto the road
they are blinded by lights

I lose count of them in radio lyrics
"I want to see Jesus on the Midnight Special
I want to see Wolfman bring him on
I want to see Jesus on the Midnight Special
That's what will help this world along"

It's the trucks that do it most
crunching them flat that way
If not trucks then it may be me
as I glide along encased in black
over the bodies of killed lovers
or killed friends and strays
without ever hearing the tire thumps
or feeling the thud
"I want to see Jesus on the Midnight Special
And hear him sing my favorite song"

SHOCK THERAPY

I used to be crazy
Didn't see in clear focus
The way the others did

Feeling it much too keenly
Bleeding from the razor word
I damn near killed myself
Gave it a glorious try

A machine reshaped me
Kcct - kcct - kcct
Kcct - kcct - kcct
Every other morning for twenty-four
Prior to a lavish breakfast

At first I was dancing happy
Memory shattered or gone
Laughing at the fragments

Then I learned to dread
Strained against the straps
Against the circle of passive faces
While no one heard my scream

Now I'm sane again
Whatever that means
Kcct - kcct - kcct

I creep like a ravished nun
Defiled
Crawling toward the altar
Trembling
Clutching the cross to my bosom
Kcct - kcct - kcct

GEORGE

Remember--George--think back
Listen--damn you--little brother
Remember to balance those feet together
Knees were made for turning and absorbing pain

You make excuses when you tell me
the sand's so frozen that boats won't float
that you're lost in a yellow summer prairie
somewhere praying--like hell you are

You are asleep in your closet
while the grass spider spins a new web
that rises to the morning

Now let me sing for lovers
a Hosanna for that sound rising
Sing of that naked frozen yellow
in our mother's children
who learn so slowly of their strength

NIGHTMARE ON MY WALL

Though I give blood for your woman's latest fancy
I remember her hair aflame before she was the sea

Pigeons know where to go when it rains   They stay
but my hands are like animals   twitching upon the table

Upside down   looking in the attic without a house
I dream of peacocks and crystal   and more peacocks

Birds tapdance in rainpools and splash the sun away
She bears fruit like a pear tree moving in the wind

A slender girl with curly hair   stands naked
by the rushing waters   of a sparkling stream
The manikin ladies   and the manikin men
and the manikin boy without hair   back on the shore
are doing   the same old things

Lying still is not as easy as it seems   Late night
I float like a brown fish   on the edge of a throbbing sea

IN ABSENCE OF SOMETHING KIND

I gravitate toward mountains
where I'm always alone
and don't need heroes

From here
It would be easier I suppose
to list what I would never do for you
But life is terminal
That's the crux of the problem

So I journeyed to Owl
because I'd heard he knew
Found him perched at home
Then in a blink
before I could phrase it
he flew
leaving nothing warm
where presence just had been

When next thinking on Humpty Dumpty
ask this foremost question
Where does it say that he's an egg

Let history be forewarned
I'm considering the possibility of foul play

MY BROTHER HAS GONE FOR HELP

I have been gored by a bull
Tossed in the air
High tumbling
Above spread-razor horns

Earlier
In a softer time
I sheltered a trio of wild rabbits
Whose mother was killed by my mower
Fed them on milk from doll bottles
Angling just so to prevent pneumonia

One by one they stiffened
In their grass-filled box
Away from the hot water bottle
Away from the ticking copper clock
The oozing milk
Away from me

Each advanced
After its interval
Into the plastic moment of death

I have been gored by a bull
A squint-eyed bull
While no one applauded
Or even watched
Beneath a white-hot sun

SUMMER FESTIVAL

That July city summer
I wore a gray felt gambler's vest
With flat pearl buttons

There were wings of blackbirds
Encircling my bare feet
And a school of stingrays
Between me and the sun

At parties women strolled up
Just to stroke their fingers
Across my bearded cheek

At night I could not sleep
Had not slept since April
So I walked alone
Belched fire at the heavens
Scuffed the sidewalk
Spat wherever I pleased

In the absence of something
I could say that there are trees
But there are no trees
I clasp firmly
There are not trees
Gnaw their bark
Are no trees
Root with them
To trees
Thrusting upward
Trees

GRAVEYARD ON CEDAR KEY

I kneel on drifted sand
to plant roses round your hill
Rich red for remembering
those long breaths you took
sliding through your teeth
like blades against my spine

We bury here above the ground
in risen mounds of oyster shells
surrounding that winding path
we walked a rainy Sunday
when a mist rose off the water
and brought your fear to stay

I lose myself this moment
as a net of dark gray light
gathers atop the stunted trees
to pull me far inside myself
It binds me to your chill

NO FAULT

I do not want your dead fish
in the middle of my rug that way
or atop the bar to remind me

Nor can your live fish swim the tub
at our soap-slippery feet dancing
Not there or anywhere else
I want that thing back in its creek

Now I must say this to you in warning
If you hang your dead fish from the ceiling
like a mobile one more time I'll scream
so loud the house will break apart

Tell you what I'd really like just now
Take that stinking fish of yours
and stick it in that slit of a pocket
that open one you are so careless with
and there it can stay and stay and stay

PALM BEACH IN AUGUST

A line of red Volkswagens
Leaves the thin black highway
And climbs white pines
To hide beneath the needles

The way things shift so sudden
Like women and thick weather

Teakettles will not pour
And time fills up my throat
With sour honey

Old women with red hair
White breasts and thighs
Fat enough to love a sailor with
Scratch painted fingers quick
Across the glare of broken shells

Close to the naked tourists
Sea birds run in circles
And dare not lift their wings

The tower with a broken bell
Hangs against a swollen sky

When the tides run backward
And sea oats flame like candles
It's best to hug your saucers
And bolt tight all the doors

NO ONE DANCES AT BREAKFAST ANYMORE

A general heaviness As of rocks Muddy-red rocks
Hanging over the interstate Ready-to-slide rocks
Cape Cod rocks Smooth-worn so as fun to finger-
feel People-tall rocks imported by architect for
neighbor's frontyard Small pebbly Myrtle Beach
rocks Held beneath tongue to taste their layered
salt Male rocks jangling nightly at breath beat
And throughout daylight following Very tiny rocks
in jewelry store case Tray-splendor of spread color
Rocks I threw at my sister and always missed except
once Ghost rocks hiding in thick grass to break
blade of my mower Sparkle rocks upon her many
playful fingers Flat slab rocks in new cemetery
that dip away from eye No rocks upon her folded
ivory fingers Gray rocks thrusting from walled-in
cemetery behind old church Molten rocks smoking up
from ocean to form hard islands Rocks remain
Private in their heaviness And no one dances
at breakfast anymore

ALONE IN MONROE PARK

There's a certain youness in the air
and my oldest everything is dead
when I turn inside to find
that it's all mixed up in me

Stone ringforts unrelenting
peat bogs which stretch forever
a woman's hand behind a rowing boat
sheep watching from a hillside
like dead men in worn blankets

Strange how fall and winter
wear each other's clothes
and how the cold--the cold
has pulled me into this

I float-dream of warmer times
of red hair spread across
the white breasts of a woman
who loved rich whiskey
and sometimes a lean sailor

But here in Monroe Park
I drink muscatel with winos
My coat is thinner than paper
my skin a crusty brown
and when I wake to the cold
my summer eyes are gone

TOGETHER THEY RAKED THE LEAVES TODAY

Blood pumps from here
to there and back again
as Willie Hampton slumps
from chair edge to tiled floor

His half-glasses half-slide
from his half-face below
my own eyes fixing down
upon an untied string
trailing a black silence
across his muddy shoe

His daughter next room over
touches herself slowly
in layers of pleasure until
she rises from chair edge
to curl on a couch below

My own eyes fix down
on brown hair in strands
damp across her curving neck
Her breath is held--released
in rainbow-skins of light

WINTERY COLLAGE

Sour gasses rise slowly
from a sour stomach
filling up the throat
and seeping through the lips
below the coppered eyes
as a body putrefies
from its own treason

A silence within bones
when I lean to open up
a letter from my dead father
who kept an untamed lady
that snarled and licked at me

When I walk without you
your letter in my pocket
I cast black shadows
deep into a swollen sky

Later as I lunch and listen
four small brothers whine
while nibbling french fries
from their fat-fat fingers
and their tall sleek mother
says shut up or I'll kill you
dead-dead one by one

Please father come back
and climb into the loft
where sweet hay is forever
where birds lay speckled eggs
and life is real as a blind man
on a nearby squalid street

IV. SUSAN (WOMAN)

SUSAN ARRIVING

On a hot July at noon
Her young ass swivels
Like a live thing on rubber bands
As she steps upon her skateboard
To pump up speed
With the piston of her golden knee

She crests the hill and soars
Arms crossed beneath tiny breasts
Black hair long in streamers
As she glides with swerving birds
Over trees and streams and mountains
To the distant valley of the lake

There she plunges downward
Beneath the water without sound
Surfaces at the lake's center
Where she floats and bobs unseen
Arms and legs spread-eagled
As she throbs to the pulse of the sun

SUSAN IN THE SPOTLIGHT

Front-page bold type
Told of her night burning
Of how she stood floodlighted
And dropped her twenty-month old
From a third-story window
To the ring of yellow firemen
Who yelled her to jump
Within their outstretched net

She could not go
Where birdsongs hover
Thicker than trees
Where light rays splatter
And hide in grass

Climbed across windowsill
Till she squirmed her body out
To fasten herself stark
Naked against wall side
And when smoke-flame closed
She would not loose her fingers

She could not go
Where birdsongs hover
And hide in grass

Family and friends talked it
That she feared the heights
Was unable to look or leap
Secure against scorching bricks
So naked that May night
While her mother remembered
That she had never climbed trees
When the other kids did
That she was raised up modest
After the ways of the Lord

She could not go
Where light rays splatter
And hide in the grass

Now white in lurid photo
Spread open for sleepy eyes
In the thick Sunday paper
Frozen by tender fingers
At lower corner of page
She clings to where she can not go

SUSAN'S LOFT

On a pale afternoon
I catch an old fear
between quick hands
and hold it in a fountain
where icelight trickles

You offer me closeness
Beneath your lifted shirt
a sharing behind green drapes
I have seen too many times
in far-off rooms like this

You go upstairs to your loft
where the bed is too high
where joy peaks to a ceiling
where it sweats of cold nights
and long-remembered hours

When I touch your palm
soft as an April rose rising
in creamy waves of light
I grow tall and bold
I am the man who ate the sun

SUSAN REACHING

She is looking for soft hands

Shielded from surfaces we move
And smoke has come between us
When we see the yellow snake

Eagle and stone can mate
When eagles have their wings clipped
They take seclusion on stone

Perched upon this high alone
I do not know what's left to eat
In the corner of my mouth or mind

In sleep I remember that nothing stays
That it cycles away--except for
This sunscorcher upon my edges
This yellow snake for her

Christ--I think--can't keep
Being everybody to her somebody
So when I finally tell her
That I love the seashore
She damn near drowns herself

She is free and wild
And looking for soft hands
I do not have--my talons
In a vision that I never was

SUSAN UPON HER BED

Her arms were flailing high
Talking to her empty room
Describing trees of other autumns

And the Chinese elm
Outside her bedroom window
Waved its yellow limbs
Fusing with her movement

That last spring by the tree
When she had stopped to lean against it
Listened to its birdsongs
Then hugged it like a child

Now she moved toward coldness
Blanketed by quick breaths
Ready to drop with the next leaf
While the tree clawed at her windowpane

They stood waiting outside her door
Speaking in reverent sounds
Their clusters of shuffling feet
Solid as a cool-maturing forest

She waved her arms once more
Before letting them fold softly
In a cross upon her pale-pink gown
Atop the stillness of her chest

SUSAN ON THE BEACH

You came to me half-afraid
So we planted a bloodstone
And watched ourselves grow

You said
"Teach me not to lie
Your tongue is strange
Your dreams are baroque
Is this all you have for me"

Then I said
"Maybe you want too much
You're not alone--babycakes
When you fear a pathless sky
And tag after the blazers"

Our early days
Sipping butterfly blood at noontime
Eating dreambread with a tipsy pilot

That first time
When the sky spoke to us
When our moorings snapped
And we lost our drift

Love is amulet
And now they wait again for us
Bluer waters with whiter beaches
Breakers that leap to the sun

SUSAN BENEATH HER WITCHMOON

Twisting on her big brass bed
She turns upon her side
Her cheek across her palm to watch
The chintz curtain blowing loose

Stretched atop the black sheet
Stroking the smoothness of satin
She lies green-eyed and white-naked
As the panther nears her footrail

He licks the toes of her feet
Climbs out the night window
Trails off into high grass
Pads back to take his stance again

The trainer faces her dresser
Rigid in the silver-braided hat
He watches the two in a smoky mirror
Holding a whip he never cracks

Centered among the four brass posts
Touching the panther with fingertips
While the moon floats red and full
She watches the open window

SUSAN UPON THE ROCK

The stroking arm of the wind
Was lusting tall to touch
Where mallards flew
Above its stretching fingertips

The Chinese elm was filigree
With Japanese beetles coupled
Feasting upon each other
While feeding on its leaves

She stood upon a rock near the tree
The wind strong in her face
Her hair blowing straight back
A long skirt swirling her thighs

Lifting the rifle
She fired it straight up
Again and again and again
Till she punctured a small cloud
And the rain poured down in rivulets
Into her upturned throat

SUSAN'S BIRTHDAY PARTY

They dance in a red cloud
With one hand over their ear
Up and down the staircase
One hand over their eye
And one hand reaching
For my gentle throat

Like the thick river
Creeping toward its ocean
Everything returns to me

Notice the table of plenty
Squirrels eat all the kernel
And the hull of a kernel of corn
When first they begin to gnaw
But after their bellies swell
They pluck the sweet nib
And cast the rest away

Warming myself at your fire
Hulls like sawdust beneath my feet
I grow fat and sleepy
There'll be blood on your walls tonight
Once my chin is on my chest
Like a chubby squirrel
My blood

SUSAN AT THE GATE

I begin to burn just now--fire-flaked
I am wrapped in a pink dressing gown
For them to turn my marble into ashes
Urn-trapped on your mantlepiece

Father you tell me there are
No snails in the garden
Eating my leaves from underneath
No yellow snails at all
Yet I am consumed by yellow
Trembling here beside you

Earlier you spoke of knights and dragons
Of gap-toothed witches with scraggy hair
And I wish my own hair was longer
When the breeze blows through
So it could flow like a mane upon it

Roaches are swarming up my back
Alive with crawlings you cannot see
Let me warn you
Snails are silent
Practising their yellow magic
While I grow smaller and smaller

If you would reach out
And put me in your trousers
With keys and coins and jangly things
Or tuck me inside your vest
In that little slit across from the watch
Where it's soft-snug and silent
As roaches or snails or the flow of yellow

I burn brightly now
Fire-flaked by intense heat
Deep inside your velvet pocket

V. MEDLEY

AUDREY

On the Beach

A young girl fronts the grain alone
with the wind alive in her hair
barefooted on coarse brown sand
where the ocean lip slides in
toward seawalk and rock pools

She strides to her secluded place
and turns within on this desolate stretch
lost in thought as she firms her pace

At Home

She reaches toward the end of her room
where her uncle has come from the dead
to perch in his chair to comfort her
until she lunges and touches air

And later with a dead father
whose staunch presence in the room
so fills it that the flees
unable to bridge an ungraced space between

At the Hospital

A woman fronts the grain alone
walks soft-shoed through glassy halls
to an dying man so charmed
by the green of her grace
that daily he sits alone to wait

"Do you want to see the fish"
and they go at his slow pace
armlocked and hips touching
to the lobby's lighted tank

From rock pools below time
an ancient fish rises into light
and the man points with glee

He returns to his crowded ward
and she bridges and strides the hall
on the graced sands of her private place

On Mountain Lake

Far above this strangely cratered lake
four hawks swoop in blackness
but a fifth hawk glides alone
over the lodge and ridging crest
Suddenly he shifts in flight
to range beyond the icy lake
remembering what he did not know he knew

Later in a cold gray fog
when she climbs the path to Bald Knob
greenness is full around her

A splotch of quick sun
on the flame of wild azeleas
hides deep inside a tree

At the top she stands on a ledge
and peers through layered haze
more ghostly than a winter moon

Her hands clutch in the wind push
fixing this moment like rock
as she looks down to see the fifth hawk
back in a time before man was

With the Hospice

She hears it during the night
with a darting movement of bird
eying each new sound arising
that a man has lately gone from her

With grace and love she hears
all that there is and more
as she cringes in a cold knowing

She first meets them stout
in fine clothes that drape and wrap
the skeletons only she can see
slinking off to wither
and lose their tufted hair

With time they shrink and break
from an ungraced pain that spreads
and wings through night air
screaming against an empty sky
to startle her from restless sleep

At Dawn

Before the dawn she stirs in sleep
flexes and rises in softness
as she waits in silence for light to flow

Now the hazel eyes are opened
with a toss of hair finer than breath
clean and pure as an ancient stone

A rebirth of grace on the wings of light
as she murmurs the warmth of waking
and opens her hand to a lifted sky

MIDNIGHT AT NO-NAME TAVERN

Glorious sunsets lately
Most beautiful fall in years
Or so I've been told
Too rushed to soak them up

Might just wait till later
When I can do it in style
Pie in my left hand for eating
And cotton-candy in my right

When I sneeze it will rain torrents
When I cough it will thunder
If I dangle my toes in the oceans
Towns will be washed away

That's the way I see it now
Though a midget has strange visions
Alone in a nameless tavern
Especially when drunk at midnight
Because I am used to looking up
Except at dogs and critters like that

BEYOND EDEN

I tuck in my navel
Savor my body juices
Intent as a crouched cat
Feeling good

After I pluck it
From the low crooked limb
It slides down my throat
Like the voice of God

Violins at candlelight
As it flows my bloodstream--
For desert I eat fig leaves

Now comes the surf
Pounding shock waves
Which toss me end over
Stronger than a winter sunrise
With its orange glow shaping
Lifting a long finger
Above a black-toothed sky

BLIND PETE'S DIORAMA

She hustled bushwackers
from dusk to yellow dawn
and she sang soprano
while no one listened

He wrestled water buffaloes
for a random sort of living
and sent checks to Elizabeth
his aging Eastern mother

Between her songs
she teased them all
timid souls or grizzly bears
in her cream-colored-wasp-waisted
low-cut satin gown
dragging the sawdust floor

They met one June
They vibed in tune
For she was some sort of woman
worth locking with
and he a leather kind of man
worth a deeper knowing

It was an old-style wedding
astride barebacked horses
with their noses pointed west
toward Red Gulch Ridge
and a blanket on a sandy dune
with miles of dark between

COLLAGE NUMBER FIVE

Walking the sidewalk together
Chomping on banana popsicles
Her arm circling his waist,
"H - m - m" he said "Black"

It was winter by the color of the sky

The old man went for one year
without a drink before he died
For whatever good it did

His wife quit hating the world
because the world was people
and people didn't deserve it

She knew it was winter by the color

Hating wrinkled her face and his face
Not the faces of the couple on the sidewalk

Tossing the stick into a rusty can
"Black" she said "You're right about that"

They knew it was winter

His wife buried him in sunglow
Carved nothing on his stone

He knew

THE HUNT

I called over the names
Of my favorite animals
Half in my sleep and half out
And cried when I remembered

Rain on the roof above me
Thumped against the tin
In a long-night reminder

I squirmed deeper
Into the featherbed
Secure-soft against tomorrow's hunt
When I would trudge off at dawn
A twelve-year-old with three uncles
For Thanksgiving with my gamebag

Tomorrow would be cold lumpy
With the blood and pulsebeat
Of dying animals touching my thigh
Half in my sleep and half out
I called their names
And felt them flutter against me
Deep in the folds of my featherbed

EULOGY

They whispered in the hallway
About what the collar hid
And none forgot it near the bier
When leaning over him to stare

Knowing what was expected of her
His own wife began
"Remarkable thing" she said
"His eggs were four minutes precisely
Harry was most insistent about that"

His sister hooked her arm
"Since he was a boy I remember
A half spoonful in every cup of coffee
Not more and not less
Or he could not bear to taste it
'Had to cut the bitter edge'
He always said"

"Indeed he was particular" the wife affirmed
"Not peculiar really
But demanding in his taste
Careful to execute each act just so
Shaved five times exactly with one side of a blade"

GOLD RECORD

He struts to the front of the stage
Prances and preens in red flickers
Tossing the mike back and forth
From hand to upturned hand
With love
Trailing the cord between shimmering legs
Sliding up and down upon it
While teenaged girls in flat haltertops
Scream in chorus for him to never stop
Lunge above the security guards
And stretch to touch his glitter.

The trouble with Rome was
That the Romans drank water from lead pipes
Till they became sterile over the years
While African slaves were boated in to breed
Not black like they ought to be
Cause the sun was cooler back then
Just kept on importing slaves
And kept on drinking out of lead pipes
Till the Empire fell--swoosh--bam
Flat from its boot
To its tail

So it isn't decadence after all
Or sex or circuses
Or a super-soft life
It's really the lead pipes
Tossing the mike from hand to hand
That will get you in the end
With love

DECEMBER PIT STOP IN A MOUNTAIN TOWN

That's the third one now
whut has broke a laig
on the ice this morning he said
taking my twenty for gas
and turning off the radio
in his glass-island room
so like a stove in winter's land

Best we get with it he said
and sport them decorations up
high on the poles for the wind to blow
Best not to go out hunting
and break a laig on ground like this
If I was much sicker he said
wiping his nose on the back of his hand
I'd need to be in bed with a nurse

Oyez oyez oyez
The king is coming to our town
to walk on a silvered street
where fire hydrants wear silly hats
and blind men sell hot tacos
to old ladies with gloved hands

BESIDE A MOUNTAIN STREAM

Watching Little Stoney
on this early spring day
where it cascades
down from White Top
across a massive boulder
evolving as sculpture
among lesser river rocks
and rising into light
half out of the cold water
knowing of pine trees
before men came to walk
stark in its splendor
so lyric in its watersound
against a morning sun

THE SUITOR

Margaret why hold yourself
from this man's newest fancy
and chill the quick slanting
of a hand that wants to please

Oh do not look at me that way
with those lined lips twitching
and trembling and clamping down
Don't hide in your recent fear

You have so strange a neck
So thin with your head cocked
like a wren too timid
to try the food of my hand

Come now away my love
from the long marbled waiting
to the trust of my reaching
and the arc of a lifted sky

Margaret I speak to you
of a time that's ripe for plucking
swollen as a ruffled bird
on the crest of a risen sea

THE SPIDER

The spider glides from a gray corner
Floats toward her pillow

She wears earplugs
Earmuffs against her screams
Sunglasses and a pale-pink blouse

Notice her wet circles at armpit
The heavy quiet of the blue carpet
The double thickness of purple drapes

She wears fur mittens and leather boots
Her comforter is white satin
The black spider is naked

Notice the spider

CONVERGING

It is a somewhat random
sound of scratching--like bone
caught within my throat
A wind sound
of me lifting your hair
in slow fingerfulls so long
and full against an open sky

It is your voice at work in me
A layered sound that rolls
rises and lilts just now
as you lean over the tub
to finger-test your water

It is something rich in sound
shimmering in a thick brown towel
tucked beneath the armpits
as I study you in shadows
beneath a closed and fallen sky
and listen to your fleshboned voice

TUXEDO IN THE ATTIC

Everything in its place
Its dusty hour

I've spent my life
Saying goodbye
To all the its
That once were vital to me

One at a time
Till all that's left is me
Sweating in the desert
Throwing kisses
To far-off mountains

I bow and close the lid
With musty grace

ABOUT THE AUTHOR

William M. White was born and grew up in Nashville, Tennessee. He received his B.A. and M.A. from Vanderbilt University and his Ph.D. from the University of Florida. His three children have followed careers in the arts. Bill is an organist, composer, and music teacher; Gail Scott is a New England abstract sculptor in Boston; Carol Ann is a poet and teacher.

The author is Professor of English and Coordinator of the Creative Writing Program at Virginia Tech in Blacksburg, Virginia. He has published scholarly and critical articles on American literature in *Forum*, *Sewanee Review*, *Studies in Short Fiction*, *Thoreau Journal Quarterly*, etc.; has published numerous short stories in magazines such as *Carolina Quarterly*, *Forum*, *Nimrod*, *Northwest Review*, *Southwest Review*, etc.; and has edited a literary magazine, *Maelstrom*.

During the last fifteen years, approximately three hundred of his poems have appeared in over one hundred and forty different quarterlies, reviews, and literary magazines. During the last five years, his poetry has been published most often in *The Southern Reivew*. He is an advisory and contributing editor to the *New Virginia Review* and has given poetry readings at numerous colleges or universities and in 1980 for the South Atlantic Modern Language Association in Atlanta.

Books:

All Nature is My Bride, Chatham Press, Old Greenwich, Conn. (1975). 146 pp. Cloth and Paper. (Introduction by Annie Dillard and illustrations by Mary Lee Herbster). This book, a selection of found poems arranged from Thoreau's *Journals*, was a choice of the Quality Paperback Division of the Book of the Month Club.

Sweet Wild World, Charles River Books, Boston, Mass. (1982). 184 pp. Cloth and Paper (Introduction by Steve Adams and illustrations by Georgia Dearborn).

From the Porch, Chase Ave. Press, Winter Park, Florida (June 1983), (A chapbook of poetry--30 pages).

ABOUT THE ILLUSTRATOR

Born in 1943 in New Jersey, I have been a resident of Blacksburg, Virginia since 1966. I attended college at Virginia Tech, where I received my undergraduate degree in Fine Arts in 1973 with a specialization in Painting, Graphics and Printmaking.

Over the years I have shown in many local art shows and University exhibitions in and around the Blacksburg and Roanoke area and have been represented at Block Prints Gallery in Blacksburg. As a result, my work is a part of several private collections. I have worked extensively, 1962 to 1984, in the commercial aspects of Graphics and Designs by doing posters and brochures for local theatre conpanies and other organizations. During this period I became involved with *Maelstrom,* a literary magazine published by the University English Department. In my first venture with a commercial publication, I contributed cover designs and illustrations for several years.

I am presently divorced and living quietly and working as a hospital attendent for the Student Health Service at Virginia Tech. I still do some painting from time to time.

John Aracco

DRAGON'S TEETH PRESS

***Living Poets' Series* (Selected Titles):**

Gustav Davidson, *All Things Are Holy*
Cornel Lengyel, *The Lookout's Letter*
Madeline Mason, *Sonnets In A New Form*
Bernard Grebanier, *The Angel In The Rock*
Thomas Thornburg, *Saturday Town*
Vasanti, *Mandala* 2^5
Madeline Gleason, *Selected Poems*
Sarah Lockwood, *New Lyrics*
Wallace Winchell, *The House of Bethlehem*
E.M. Schorb, *The Poor Boy*
P.B. Newman, *Paula*
Ray Staszko, *The Last Fiddler Crab*
Robert L. Smith, *Refractions*
Doreen Gandy, *Poems for Twelve Moods*
Dorsha Hayes, *New Poems from the Bell-Branch*

DRAMA:

The Devil Comes to Wittenberg by George Hitchcock. Prize Play, New Poetic Drama, Vol. 1. $3.50.

MUSIC (for voice and piano):

Fifty Songs by Ernst Bacon, with introduction by Paul Horgan. $5.
Hesperides by John Edmunds. Great Lyrics set to music. $10.
Selected Songs by Jeanne Singer. $7.50.

PHILOSOPHY:

The Creative Self by Cornel Lengyel.
Aspects of the artist's quest for self-knowledge and the springs of creativity. $5.
"One of the best books on creativity ever written."

—*Corinne Geeting, WEST/ART*

Order from

DRAGON'S TEETH PRESS
El Dorado National Forest
Georgetown, California 95634